THE GOD WHO ANSWERS BACK

REAL MIRACLES AS REPORTED
BY EVERYDAY PEOPLE

COMPILED BY

Mark Aho

(Miracles provided by God)

CONTENTS

Introduction

Is God still alive? If God be with us, where are the miracles? Many people look with quiet longing upon the stories of past ages. Even those who doubt that God performs miracles today might secretly wish he would. But could it be that the presumption that He does not can blind us to the fact that He may indeed be doing so—just outside of our scope of vision? There are many things people believe in with no firsthand experience. How many people believe in alligators, even though they have never seen one? They just understand that the alligators exist somewhere, personal experience notwithstanding. Would we not consider the person rather odd who insists, until I SEE an alligator, I do not believe they exist? Sounds kind of silly, doesn't it? But those who have never witnessed a real miracle firsthand could be tempted to take that kind of a view. Could it simply be that—for whatever reason—they were in another place when the miracle happened? We respectfully request that each reader consider that possibility.

The stories reported in this book are true, and were sometimes the pivot point where life and death converged for the people who tell them. Having experienced such intense drama with life hanging in the balance, the thought that God performs no miracles is fully and permanently banished from their minds. They have SEEN the alligator, so to speak. But, to carry the example further, the chance to see that animal is greatly increased if one is willing to travel to where they are said to be. Those who review a Broadway play go to Broadway to watch it. It is specific ACTION that brings a person into a position to be a firsthand witness.

For the people in this book, it may have been the desperation of having no other answer that forced them to take those actions. But similar actions CAN be taken by people who are NOT in desperation. For these, the miracles of God are witnessed simply because they are willing to see them, and are paying attention. He who would please God must believe that "He IS, and He is a rewarder of them that diligently seek Him" (Hebrews 11:6). If that is true of God's person, might it also be true of His acts? We think so, and these testimonies are written to inspire you to come to the place where you also may witness a miracle.

Mark Aho

2022-2023

The Shalom Boyer Story

Surgery Cancelled!

Six year old Shalom Boyer was the cheerful beloved daughter of Darren Boyer and his wife Damaris, living in Grande Prairie, Alberta. Darren was the pastor of a small church in that town. But suddenly, something was very wrong with Shalom. For two weeks, she was deathly sick. Her right eye became slow. Also her right hand and her right foot would drag when she walked. There was a flu going around, but these were strange symptoms of a flu. Finally, her parents took her in to the emergency where a CT scan revealed a problem in her brain. The doctor's comment was, "90% of the cases that come into emergency are not urgent, but this IS urgent." She was immediately flown to Edmonton to see a neurosurgeon. It turned out that a whole team of them were waiting, including the head of the department.

Further tests confirmed a large tumor on the right side of Shalom's brain. Including surrounding affected areas, the mass appeared to her father to be nearly the size of his closed fist-- a massive area for a child that size. The doctors emphasized the seriousness of the case. It was not an aneurysm, it was a tumor, and the pressure was so intense that even a sneeze could cause it to erupt into bleeding. If that were to happen, surgery would need to start within 10 minutes, or permanent brain damage would occur.

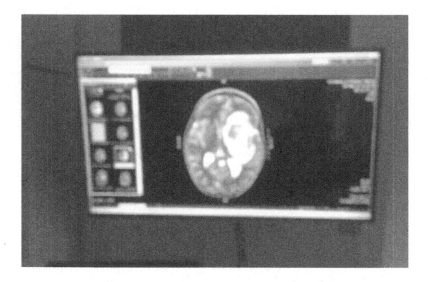

Shalom needed to be kept calm and still while preparations for a series of surgeries were made. The Boyers were warned that the tumor could be cancerous, but even if it was not, it was possible Shalom would permanently lose speech, and the use of her whole right side.

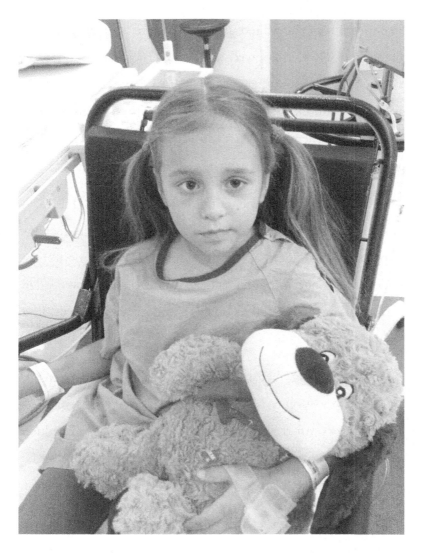

Doctors were continuously standing by in case of the need to operate immediately, while Darren and his wife tried to keep

Shalom calm as she waited in intensive care. But that was not all they did. They also prayed, and passed the prayer request on to others who knew them, and knew the power of God to intervene. Church members and other pastors began to pray, even through the night. One pastor texted in that all the young people in his church were praying.

That night, Darren was not able to sleep much. His head was pounding, and it was hard to think clearly. Guilty feelings crept in as he wondered if it was all his fault for failing to take Shalom in sooner. Though in a dazed state, he knew he needed a miracle, and would occasionally wonder, what exactly IS a miracle?

That morning, before 8:30 am, Shalom needed to go through a pre-surgery MRI test without moving. Darren was on hand to comfort Shalom before the 30-minute procedure. However, Shalom was in such a lifeless state she could not be anything but calm. Darren describes those moments this way:

"I stood in the same room as our daughter lay in that machine. In that room with the nurse doing the test behind a glass wall to my back, I believe the Lord met our daughter. While she was laying in the MRI and I was standing alone in that room, it was like a presence was there and I

was allowed to fellowship with that presence. I can't say I was praying or thinking deeply. As the machine made its noises, making a back and forth sound, I thought maybe it was because they couldn't find the tumour? It was like this hope I had and it seemed like a child-like faith, thinking it was the sound of a machine looking, but not able to find anything wrong."

The MRI test did go on unusually long. What exactly happened in those moments, as Darren stood by and the MRI machine hummed along, examining his daughter? This was an urgent situation requiring immediate medical intervention. Multiple tests, doctors, and top neurosurgeons, some of the best in the field, all testified to that. There was no doubt about the case. This final MRI was just for surgery prep. Actually, the MRI was unusually long because a second MRI test was immediately undertaken. Why? What was happening? Darren describes what happened next:

"About 11 am, back in intensive care, the team of neurosurgeons arrived. They asked if we wanted to see the results of the recent scan. As those 3 surgeons discussed the situation and were using medical terms, I asked the question based on what I was hearing. 'So my daughter doesn't need to have an operation?' The head doctor looked at me and said no, "I believe this is all blood and she will heal from that." As they continued

their open discussion, it was more than I could bear. I stepped away a short distance and began to praise God under my breath for it seemed so certain her entire condition had changed."

Whatever happened in those moments under the MRI machine, the tumor that was clearly there just hours before was now gone! The only thing that intervened between the many tests that showed it present and the MRI that showed it gone was prayer. In those moments, Darren found the answer to his question: a miracle is the presence of God. It was that presence that removed the tumor in Shalom's brain, in those moments under the MRI machine.

In the days leading up to this, Shalom had been uncomfortable, enduring intense pressure in her brain, and forced to remain in a state of stillness unnatural for an active 6 year old girl. But there in the hospital that morning, after the team of Doctors gave their review, she became alert, even hungry. Darren and his wife both testify,

"For the most part, she recovered instantly that morning. It was completely over, at least as far as I believed and she demonstrated...she began to move, to laugh, and a sweet spirit seemed to be present in everything she did and said. The nurses said they had never seen a little

girl in intensive care eat so much!"

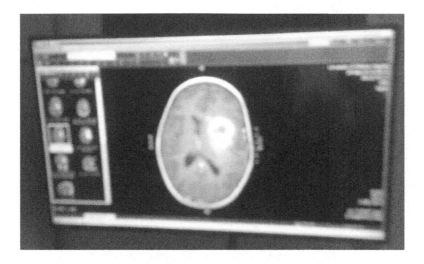

A couple of days later, a camera scope was run up her leg and into her brain in the hopes that this might provide some explanation for what had happened. There was no explanation. When everything was found normal, the head neurosurgeon confessed, *"What happened to your daughter is pretty miraculous."* Doctors aren't taught terms like "miraculous" in medical school. But sometimes, medical terminology just does not fit the case.

Over the next little while, Shalom recovered just as the doctor predicted. An MRI several months later confirmed that there was no lingering problem. Her brain is now so completely normal that the doctors require no further examinations.

Let's use the doctor's term, and call it a miracle. The miracle that happened to Shalom Boyer did not happen in a secret dark corner. Doctors saw it--in fact, the whole medical system witnessed it, as the neurosurgical team had been alerted to action. Many Believers, including whole churches, were praying. All of these are witnesses to the before, during, and after of another instance of The God Who Answers Back.

Darren and Damaris Boyer and family. Shalom is in the back row center.

Healthy Shalom Today with Mother, Damaris

Ruth Garland

Healing Before the Doctors Arrived

Preacher Darrell Ward is no stranger to the miraculous acts of God. The amazing recovery of his daughter, Jessica, following a deadly car accident is featured in this book on page 61. In addition to being a preacher, Darrell is a medical professional, and is well acquainted with both the wonders and the limits of what human intervention can do.

Through the years, Darrell has continued to boldly preach and testify to the miraculous power of God around the world, and has personally witnessed many miracles.

On May 24, 2023, at a Wednesday night service at Word of Life Tabernacle in Johnson City, Tennessee, Darrell was in the middle of preaching on the subject of the miraculous power of God. It was in this very service, under the hearing of this topic, that a woman in the back suddenly collapsed! Her daughter who was nearby caught and held her limp body as she emitted the gurgling sound known as "agonal breathing," common in cardiac arrest.

Bro. Darrell Ward Preaching

The woman, Ruth Garland, was not a visitor. She was

known to many in the congregation and had attended that church for years. Therefore the before, during, and after of this situation happened fully in the open before people in the best of all positions to evaluate it.

Several people in the building had medical training, and they all confirmed that the woman had no pulse. Yet, the congregation remained calm. The service was being video recorded at the time. In the video, you can see Darrell pause in his preaching, and alert the pastor that someone was sick. He left the platform, and he and pastor Donny Reagan went to pray for the woman. The camera remained on the platform, but you can hear a calm prayer--unusually calm, considering the circumstances. A few minutes later, Darrell returned to the platform and finished his preaching, assuring the congregation that the woman would be alright.

Those near the event testify that as the prayer went forth, Ruth Garland immediately regained consciousness, and was perfectly fine from that moment. Ruth's brother-in-law texted this report the following day:

"I truly believe I witnessed a miracle at church as you prayed. Ruth was "out of it" and maybe even dead. She was lifeless and it looked as

though she had passed. As you prayed, she came to life...almost immediately, she regained consciousness and was coherent. I believe and so does Wanda, we witnessed a miracle right before our very eyes. God bless you."

Ruth's daughter also texted in this report:

"Good morning brother Darryl, I brought Mom home at 5:30 this morning, they did a CT scan, normal! Chest x-ray, normal! Blood work, normal! Sugar slightly elevated, no dehydration, blood pressure a little high. The doctor actually had no explanation for what happened but I know God showed up! I know what I saw, I know what I heard, and I know God showed up. Thank you for your prayers. I appreciate you, she is doing very good. Thursday evening, sister Ruth was eating at a local restaurant with no memory of what happened. Our God is awesome. He opens the eyes of the blind and raises the dead to life."

The service where this took place is viewable in its entirety on the church website archives for that date.

Some cases where God intervenes are replete medical records because the situation has progressed to the point where they are available. But in this situation, there are none, simply because the issue was fully resolved before a doctor even got involved! Is this a lesser miracle, or is it an even greater miracle? If it were you who were sick, which would you prefer: months or years of treatment, or an immediate cure? If God can heal one person after the doctors have done all they can do, He can just as surely heal another before the doctors even arrive!

Whether it is immediate, or after some time has passed, cases like this show that God truly does answer back.

Carolyn Russell

A 12-Year Journey of Faith

Real Miracles as Reported by Everyday People

It all started with a small black mole behind my left ear. I was always trying to hide it. I never wanted people to see it. When they did, comments were made about getting it cut off. But I've always believed God is my healer.

It went from being the size of a penny to the size of a quarter. This is when someone told me it could be cancer. I do not like to go to a medical doctor. I started praying for the Lord to take it away. One evening it was really bothering me, so I asked my husband to pray with me. I told him I felt like my skin had been plagued. The next morning, I took my Bible and a cup of coffee out on my porch to have my morning reading. I had no particular place I was going to read, I just let my Bible open. It was like all the pages were black, but one scripture jumped out at me; Mark 5:34 "And he said unto her, Daughter thy faith hath made thee whole; go in peace, and be whole of thy plague." I read this over and over, rejoicing greatly, for I knew I was healed!

Jumping ahead 12 years later, I was still holding on to my promise even though things started to get worse. Only a few people knew of my struggle. Brother Andrew Coressel prayed with me many times, encouraging me to have faith.

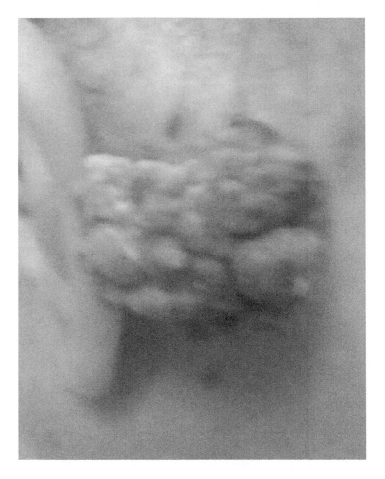

One evening in church, after the message, Brother Kidri Diggs prophesied over me, telling me that God had heard my prayers and that God was on my side; that I had pressed through my doubts, and pressed through how Satan had been fighting me. He said three times that God was on my side. This greatly encouraged me to keep holding onto my promise. I spoke to Brother Diggs about what was going on and how I was being told it was cancer. He told me to hold onto my faith. He said, "The day you go to a doctor is the day you'll have what they said!"[1] This made my faith in God's Word stronger. Many more things happened but I just kept reading my promise in God's Word.

Then things changed. It grew so big it was pressing against my ear. It became so very sore that I couldn't touch it. It would bleed if I rolled over on it in bed. At one point, I got out of bed to pray, not asking God to heal me but asking Him when. I was so desperate! All I could hear was a song like it was being sung to me, "In God's time, in His time. He makes all things beautiful in His time." I started praising the Lord. I knew He heard my cry and answered me.

August 8, 2015, Brother Darrell Ward came to minister to us. I attend Brother Ray Ericson's church in Bluffton, OH, True Word Tabernacle. At the end of the service, people were going up for prayer. I knew I should go too. I was standing in

---

[1] Evangelist Kidri Diggs has a gift of prophecy that has proven accurate on many occasions. This type of counsel may not be appropriate for every case.

my seat praying while Brother Ward was praying for someone else. I said, "Lord, I've asked for prayer so many times. I'd be ashamed to ask for prayer again." At that very moment, Brother Ward looked in my direction and said, "Christian friend, don't ever say you would be ashamed to ask for prayer." That was it! I went up for prayer, searching my heart to make sure there was nothing between me and Jesus; that all things were made right; nothing to hinder my healing. By the time Brother Ward leaned down to me for my request, I could barely speak, my heart was pounding so hard. I knew I was in the presence of the Lord! I don't remember what I said to Brother Ward, but he understood. After prayer, I was so weak I needed help to return to my seat.

The next morning nothing had changed. Day two, things were the same. Day three, I searched the message to find out all that was said about the third day, but things were the same. On the afternoon of the fourth day, it became very itchy but it was still so very sore. With my thumb, I rubbed the bottom of the area and a small piece came off. This happened a lot over the next few days until, finally, the entire thing was gone! Words could never express my thankfulness to the Lord.

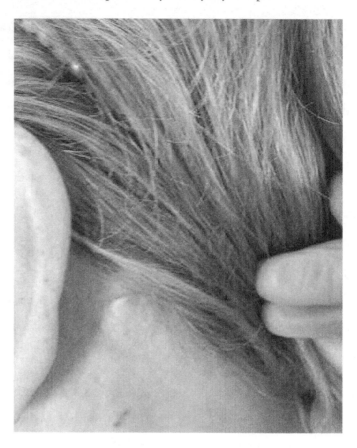

Brother David Siler was ministering at our church. I knew that he and Brother Ward were such good friends, so I went to him after service and asked him to tell Brother Ward it was gone.

I will never stop praising my Lord for touching me. Prayer indeed changes things. Our Lord is faithful.

Job Wohali

Overturning the Ultrasound Report

This is our true story of the healing of our son Job.

In the fall of 2006, we found out we were expecting our fourth child! We were so excited, and having been already blessed with three girls, we hoped this child would be a son. In January of 2007, we went in for our first ultrasound to find out the gender of our baby. Once the ultrasound was over, the doctor asked to meet with us and told us that, yes, in fact, it was a boy, however, followed with some bad news. She showed us several scans of the brain on the ultrasound, and it looked like there were empty holes on each side of his brain. The doctor told us that if we were praying people, we should really start praying. She did not provide exact details of the diagnosis but requested for us to go for further testing. We left the doctor's office in complete disbelief and heartbroken. We didn't know what to do, but we are Believers, so praying is exactly what we did.

We took our three little girls to my sister Hannah's house, and we went to our church to PRAY! We were in such turmoil, but knew God was in control, even when everything felt out of control. We wept upon our faces before the Lord at our little church until we knew the peace and assurance of the Lord and knew He was in complete control. We knew God had healed our son, and before we got up off our knees, I told my wife that our son's name would be Job. No matter what trials would ever come his way, we wanted him to be like Job of old, who never denied God.

We took these Bible promises into our hearts, believed them, and confessed them!

Isaiah 53:5 "He was wounded for our transgressions, He was bruised for our iniquities, the chastisement of our peace was upon Him, and with His stripes we are healed"

Psalms 103:3 "Who forgiveth all thine iniquities, who healeth all thy diseases."

1 Peter 2:24 "Who His own self bare our sins in His own body on the tree, that we, being dead to sins, should live unto righteousness: by Whose stripes ye were healed."

On our second ultrasound in May 2007, the doctor told us our son's brain was completely perfect! We were so thankful to the Lord. Our son was not due until July 2007, and we kept telling everyone of his healing and confessing it, no matter what Satan would try to tell us. We knew God had given us a complete healing. So when the day came for delivery, on July 12, 2007, a perfectly healthy baby boy was born!

Today, Job is a very athletic, intelligent young man. He carries a 4.0 GPA, is on track to graduate high school with his

Associates degree, trains and competes in Jujitsu, and, most importantly, loves the Lord Jesus with all his heart. He is constantly witnessing the love of God to his peers. He is a living testimony that God's promises are still the same yesterday, today, and forever.

Moses and Denelle Wohali
Athol, Idaho

Moses and Denelle Wohali and Family

Witness Testimony

In 2007, my brother and his wife Denelle were expecting their fourth child. At her first ultrasound, they were given some very concerning news. The doctor told them that something looked to be seriously wrong with the development of the baby's brain and that they'd be able to tell them more at the next scheduled ultrasound. She told them, if they were praying people, they better pray for their baby. They, along with all our family, asked God to intervene and heal the baby. I remember them dropping the girls off at my house, and they said they were going to go to our church and just lay before the Lord and cry out to Him. When they left, they were very heavy-hearted, you could just feel their pain. They were gone for hours and when they came back, I could tell their burden was lifted, they were very peaceful. They said they committed it to the Lord, and they knew He heard them and that they believed the baby would be perfectly well! At the next ultrasound, the doctor said everything looked just the way it was supposed to. Their son, Job, was born perfectly healthy and today is a strong, smart, active young man! He is a walking testimony of what the Lord can do!

Hannah Edwards, Charlestown, IN

Real Miracles as Reported by Everyday People

Witness Testimony

My husband and I were living in Montana and had become close friends with the Wohali family in Idaho. I was pregnant with our first child at the same time that Denelle Wohali was pregnant with Job. They asked us to pray as they had received some alarming news concerning their unborn baby. A few months later, a new ultrasound revealed the baby was perfectly whole. Praise God!

Ruth Greeley, Williamsburg. WV

LaDonna Smith

Given Up to Die of Covid

My name is LaDonna Smith, and this is my testimony of healing. I thank the Lord Jesus Christ for all He has done. May He receive all glory and honor for it because He is truly worthy of it all!

On Sunday, July 25, 2021, I tested positive for COVID. This was not good news, as my immune system was very compromised due to previous health challenges. The Lord previously healed me from cancer which left me without many lymph nodes, and in 2018, a near-fatal bout with bronchitis had turned into sepsis.

After testing positive for COVID, for the first few days, I felt fine but in the early hours of Wednesday morning, July 28th, I woke up having difficulty breathing and was taken by ambulance to the hospital. Sadly my husband was not permitted to go in with me due to COVID restrictions, but the Lord was my comforter and the Lord never left me.

Later that afternoon, around 4:30 pm, while waiting to be

placed in a room, I was talking to my daughter, Ashleigh, on the phone. I was in excruciating pain and told Ashleigh that my heart was beginning to hurt very badly. Ashleigh instructed me to quickly press the button that calls to the nursing station. I had no memory of the next few moments until months later.

When the nurses came into the room, I had gone into respiratory failure, but my heart never stopped beating. The nurses seemed very rushed and upset but I was suddenly in a completely different state. I felt the most wonderful feeling I have ever felt in my life. I don't know how to express, with human language, the feeling I felt at that moment. The best way to describe it is pure love. I felt the Lord holding me from behind and the most amazing love was coming from Him, which seemed to be passing through me, towards the nurses that were frantically trying to help me. He loved them so much and I just wanted to comfort them. Although I now know that I wasn't talking, I felt like I was telling them, "Look! I'm so good now! I can breathe! I have no pain!" The peace I felt was immeasurable. It was just perfect love. That is what He is and what I felt all around me. Oh, how He loves us.

What happened over the next few days, I will let my

daughter Ashleigh tell, as I was on life support while the Lord was moving on the prayers of people all over the world…

My name is Ashleigh Watts. While on the call with my mom, I heard the phone drop and footsteps scurrying around the room. Moments later, the line disconnected. I received a call about 10 minutes later from a nurse, very calmly saying that they needed to intubate my mom. Immediately, I reached out to my pastor's wife, who encouraged me and told me to put a prayer request on Facebook as well. She told me that would be a quick way to get people praying, and boy was she right. People from all over began to cry out to the Lord on our behalf. We felt the prayers almost instantly.

The next few days would be the hardest trial our family had ever gone through. My mom was now in ICU, and we were at home having to rely on phone calls to the nurse's station every shift change for updates on her condition.

We began calling from Wednesday night onwards, each time getting a more negative report. Her blood pressure dropped so low they put her on vasopressors, which are blood pressure regulators that pull the blood from the extremities to the vital organs. Each time we called, it seemed like they added another pressor and at the end of each call, it never failed to be said… *"Your mother is a very sick woman."* It was discouraging, yet our faith remained. Her blood pressure was around 34/14 and her heart rate was at 170. The doctor told us this heart rate was that of someone running a marathon for three days straight.

Thursday morning, we called at shift change and received another negative report with her declining rapidly. By Thursday afternoon, we were met with words I will never forget, *"She is a very sick woman and we will continue to work with her as long as it makes sense."* As we would get each report, I would update on Facebook. The prayers continued going up and the support continued pouring in.

 Ashleigh Watts
Just now · 🌐   ● ● ●

The doctors are not giving my sweet momma much hope through the night but we know a man who can turn on the light in our darkest night. We believe the Lord will move on the scene. If you ever prayed for us, please pray now. Pray like it was your momma. Please.

In the late hours of Friday night, we were told my mom would not make it to see the next day. When my pastor's wife heard the news, she instructed me to ask them if there was any way we could come into the hospital due to the circumstances. An exception was now made for us to go. They were allowing us to say our goodbyes. Instead of saying goodbye, we went in to have a prayer meeting.

We arrived at the hospital around midnight Friday night. My mom was swollen to almost double her size in fluid and was connected to more monitors than I could count. At this point, they had her on five pressors and her vitals were only worse. Prior they told us that they generally stop after four pressors as there is not much hope of life after that. I remember there being so many hospital staff in such a small room, whispering to one another. It seemed they were waiting for the inevitable. After much laboring over her, they were at their wit's end and could offer no other options.

My dad was on one side of her and I on the other. We squeezed her almost lifeless hands and she was not at all responsive. Immediately we got my pastor on the phone, who was waiting for our call. He began to pray over her and explained to us the great peace that he had just received. In his prayer, he told us of how the Lord told him to "Speak Life," and that is what he did. As the prayer was going forth, my mom

Real Miracles as Reported by Everyday People

began moving around in response.

We stayed at the hospital until around 4 am with our faithful family members on the phone, praying nonstop.

We were later told this was unheard of for someone with such low blood pressure to be moving at all. After the prayer, my mom began to respond to our requests. We would ask her to squeeze our hands if she could hear us, and she would muster up all the strength she had and do it. Though not seeing much change in her vitals, we left the hospital with peace, and the doctor later expressed to the nurse, *"Tonight we saw love bring someone back to life."*

The next morning when we called, they told us not much had changed but the only thing they could do was to begin weaning her off pressors, start dialysis and turn her over on her stomach. These were last-resort options. As each pressor was removed, it seemed she got better and better. With each phone call through the days following, her vitals were improving. The doctors and nurses could not believe the progress she made. Staff from all over the hospital would come by to look through the window at their "Miracle Girl."

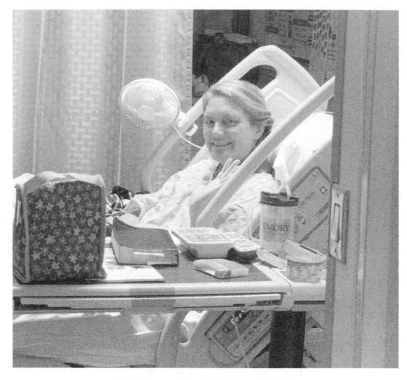

LaDonna Smith Recovering

I feel like I need to stop here and mention a few other things. Though we were beginning to see a huge miracle, the Lord was also working in every detail. Because of all the medications, many COVID patients must go on dialysis but once again, the saints went to prayer and God moved in a mighty way. You see, my mom only had one kidney, but suddenly, that one kidney began acting as two and got the job done. Isn't our God faithful? Also, they told us that because of the pressors, her toes turned black, and she would probably lose some of them. Again, with much prayer, she has ten healthy toes today.

My mom was in the hospital and in rehabilitation for 39 days. What a beautiful parallel, as Jesus took 39 stripes for our healing. The road to recovery was not quick but day by day, she would make progress in the right direction, even relearning to walk and perform daily tasks. She is a picture of health today. Praise our Lord Jesus. He is truly the same yesterday, today and forever.

We are beyond thankful for the great work the Lord did, and for everyone who prayed with us through the long days and long nights. We could not have made it through without the body of Christ.

Ladonna Smith with Husband, Chris

LaDonna Smith

A Hospital Worker Testifies

My name is Robert and I am a RN at Piedmont Athens Regional. I began my career 6 months before the Covid-19 pandemic began. During this, we witnessed so much, much of which we don't care to recall. With that being said, many of us found some goodness in all of the bad.

My goodness began one night when a lady came to the ICU and her family was close behind. Her husband was escorted by a friend of his, who I somehow recognized from many years previous. I wasn't her nurse, but assisted with care from time to time. This is the norm in the ICU, but even more so during this fragile time in medicine. I began to speak to the husband and discovered the friend was exactly who I thought it was. The husband and I didn't know each other, but we both knew a lot of the same people.

As the days and nights passed, Chris and I began to talk and a friendship blossomed. I tried to answer any questions and explain any changes in the treatment his wife received. He was always so thankful. This man stayed in the ICU as much as we would possibly allow him. If he wasn't there, their daughter Ashleigh was. This angel-like soul stood at her momma's door and prayed and talked to her mom as if she were standing right there. Ashleigh truly has the voice of an angel.

As this awful sickness continued to try to take their sweet loved one from them, LaDonna fought and she fought HARD! LaDonna continued to get worse. Her oxygen demands continued to increase while her oxygen saturation and blood pressure decreased. The doctors continued to add medications to help with her blood pressure, but to no avail, she needed more. Her body continued to fight, but her blood pressure wasn't responding to the medicine. She was on three of these medications we call "pressors." They squeeze the vasculature with the hope of increasing the blood pressure. We were on a third pressor and next to the last one we typically use. This is when I began caring for LaDonna. It was at this point, of course after some time, that the turnaround began. Slowly, LaDonna began to make the turn and the pressors began to be turned off. LaDonna was beating the odds. She continued to improve to the point all of the pressors were turned off and she was able to maintain a good blood pressure. The same thing began to happen with her oxygen demands. As the demand dropped, so did the amount of oxygen until the day she had the endotracheal tube removed. She was beating the odds because this horrible, unforgiving virus had taken so many others. During this entire time, her husband and daughter rarely, if ever, left the ICU. She was eventually transferred to the floor, where she continued to improve.

I would check on LaDonna while she was on the floor, making sure she continued to improve and made it out! She was truly one of the sickest patients we had during the pandemic that defied the odds, not only to leave the hospital, but to make a full recovery and return home to her loving family.

I was so fortunate to have been able to care for LaDonna and meet her amazing family. Chris and I continue to stay in touch. We talk about family, current events, our kids and their accomplishments and struggles. Chris just shared a video of LaDonna running, yes RUNNING!

2021-2022

Alana Butts

Healed of Cancer

"My Christmas present in December of 2017 was a diagnosis of stage 4 Classical Hodgkin's Lymphoma, with a 7 cm tumor in my lung. I had just turned 40 and had a husband and five pre-teens and teenagers.

"While this was a great shock, I began to look to God for comfort and healing, and we encouraged our family to do the same. We made a conscious decision not to fear, and the battle was on. I was to have six months (twelve treatments) of chemotherapy, with a likely possibility of radiation when that ended. I was very weak and sick before my treatment even started, and the Doctor was concerned that I would not be strong enough to endure them all. We began to pray that the Chemotherapy would go straight to its target and that side effects would be minimal.

"I experienced many dark moments during that time. I lost more weight, getting down to 95 lb. I was strengthened by the love and scriptural encouragement shown to me at that time and I looked to God for healing. It gradually became real to me that God truly is a healer, that He took stripes on His back the day He went to Calvary for my healing. I began to believe His promises, and I began to even look for a supernatural intervention. The Lord graciously heard my prayer and that of His people who were praying for me. After I had completed just four chemotherapy treatments, I had a PET Scan to determine if the Chemotherapy was beginning to work. To the astonishment of the Doctor, all traces of cancer were gone, including the 7 cm tumor in my lung. Over four years later, I am still giving glory to God for his wonderful healing touch, and for sparing me the rest of my treatments.

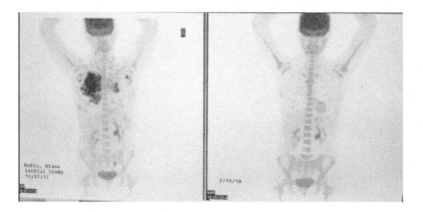

"This is just a brief summary of what happened. The complete story is so dramatic that it is in no need of embellishment to grip your heart. My life has been forever changed by this personal encounter with a Living God. If you would like to hear the complete story and see pictures and video clips, you can find it on YouTube.com by searching, "Leaning on the Everlasting Arms - The Testimony of Alana Butts" (https://bit.ly/3zlTlXJ). I believe it will encourage you to a deeper expectation of how God can move in your life."

Moriah Pruitt

Healed of Alopecia Areata

"My name is Moriah Pruitt and I am 18 years old. When I was 11, my mom found a bald spot on my head about the size of a quarter. We went to the doctors and found out that it was Alopecia Areata and there was no cure or hope of it ever growing back. They told us that they had multiple patients with alopecia and they wear wigs. They said if it did grow back, it would be white or in patches. Within a year, I was completely bald.

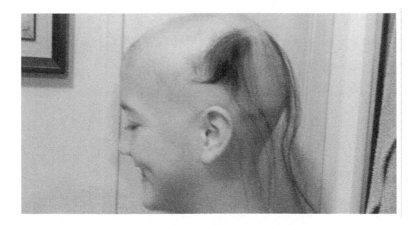

I believe in A Living God who will and does heal the sick and he took stripes at Calvary for my healing. My church puts on a youth camp every year at Easter. I carried a hairpin through the prayer line expecting and believing I would have hair to wear it. The ministers anointed me with oil and prayed for me. My confession was and always will be I can, I will, I do believe that Jesus heals me now, and in 3 months, my head was covered with hair.

"My hair has continued to grow until now, 6 years later, it has reached waist length. I continue to thank and praise my God for doing the miraculous and for healing me.

"Jesus Christ is the same Yesterday, Today and Forever.

"And I know that what He has done for me, He can do for you if you only believe and trust Him.

"For more details, the video of my testimony is on YouTube, "Restoring the Glory" (https://bit.ly/3Q83VbG)."

Jessica Ward

Healed of Critical Injuries

The story of Jessica Ward, the "Miracle Girl" from Kingsport
Tennessee.

On March 14 1995, 2 ½ year old Jessica Ward was in a
severe automobile accident in which her grandfather and aunt
were killed.

Jessica's injuries were so severe that she was not expected
to live. Her lungs were torn by contusions, her femur was
shattered, her teeth had cut through her jaw, her kidneys were
bleeding, her spleen was torn, her heart was bruised, and she

had severe brain damage.

Reports of the accident were aired on TV, and news stories of her miraculous recovery followed. Jessica's parents were told that even if she did survive, she would be blind for life, she would never walk again, never go to school, never have a normal life of any kind. But Jessica, through the prayers of many, was touched by a living God—the God who answers back. Everything that medical science said was impossible came to pass.

Today, Jessica is a healthy and thriving young woman. She graduated from high school with honors, with perfect eyesight, complete mobility, and no visible effects from the accident that left her on death's door.

See the entire story on YouTube: The Healing of Jessica Ward, (Not Yet, Daddy) - Brother Darrell Ward Testimony (https://bit.ly/3oHPaR4).

John Waldner

The Miracle of a Changed Life

"Being born and raised in a home where I was under the influence of Christian teachings, taken to church and taught the things of the Lord, I grew up as a young man with no desire for that kind of life for myself.

Real Miracles as Reported by Everyday People

"The sparkle and shine of the world had caught my eye with its pleasures, while anything religion had a bitter taste to me.

"As I grew through my teenage years, I was pulled, influenced, and completely drifted into the depths of sin and ungodliness. Partying, drugs, alcohol, smoking, lying and stealing and wasting away my life was a daily activity of mine as a 16 year old teenager.

"Carrying a great burden and load of sin, at times the fear of death and hell would shake me to say a semi-sincere prayer in moments of anxiety or great pain. That was the depth of my religion.

"One day as a 16 year old; while at home with a friend that I had known my whole life from church, I was told by him some things regarding a close friend of ours. This friend of ours had also attended church with us in our childhood and went down a similar path into the depths of sin. We all walked this path of sin together.

"I was told how that through the power of a living God, our friend had been completely delivered and life supernaturally changed completely.

"As I was listening to the testimony of this man, immediately the pricks of conviction began picking at my heart. Religion and tradition had no desire in my mind but a LIVING GOD who really changes lives was certainly a desire of mine.

"From that moment, at home on my balcony, I felt the pulling and call of repentance knocking at the door of my heart.

"Being taught in my youth, I knew what I was experiencing was the conviction of the Holy Spirit. It was the Lord Jesus knocking at my heart trying to gain entrance, trying to get me to surrender my life of Sin and walk in a life free of Sin.

""If God can do it for that man, Surely God could do it for me." These were the words echoing through the corridors of my heart that night as I was resisting and trying my very best to hush that holy call.

"Eventually, through the great mercies of God, that night alone in my bedroom, I knelt over my bed in answer to the beckoning of the Holy Spirit. I cried unto the Lord and repented of all my sins and accepted the Lord Jesus Christ as my personal Saviour.

Real Miracles as Reported by Everyday People

"Rising up from prayer, I felt as though in my room the abundance of prayers that had been spoken over me through the years had just been answered.

"I went to my knees as a poor sinner boy with no hope or direction for my life, and came up from my knees completely changed on the inside. In a moment my desire for immorality, drugs, cigarettes, alcohol, and riotous living had been wiped out. I had been set free from anxiety, fears, nervousness, and pride. I began to hunger for God, righteousness, and to line up with The Bible and to please God.

"And now, 9 years later, as a 25-year-old, the testimony of Jesus Christ remains the same. I have never gone back to any of those things I once desired, nor have I been bound by the fears and anxieties that once tormented me.

"My testimony can be watched in more detail on YouTube: John Waldner Testimony Pt 1 (https://bit.ly/3zbZ4iI)."

John Waldner and Family

Emmanuel Cibasu

The Accident that Never Happened

Preacher Emmanuel Cibasu refers to John 17:9 as proof that Jesus has already prayed for his children. He believes his testimony is an example of God answering that prayer.

In a dream, Emmanuel was looking through the back window of his house, and saw one of his cars parked on the street. Suddenly he saw a rental truck coming at high speed and striking at least 8 cars, 4 on both sides of the road. The truck flew over his car, and then hit 8 more cars on the other side.

Real Miracles as Reported by Everyday People

He could see the driver of the truck and the passenger clearly. In the dream, he was the only person who saw them, and knew the location of the accident. He told his wife and children what he had seen.

The next day, his truck that he normally takes to work, did not start (Later that day, it started with no problem). So he took his car to work—the car that was in the dream!

Driving back from work, he was traveling down the 4th lane of a 5-lane highway, and the lane was slowing down. The 3 other lanes to his right were moving freely. He was listening to a recorded sermon preached by William Branham. Suddenly he heard a loud crash behind him, and he saw debris from cars flying up in the rearview mirror. Four cars were hit. The car behind him looked like it would crash into him, but it stopped within 6 inches. Cars were flying sideways, striking other cars.

Then he saw the bottom of a large truck, pass fully airborne over his car. It landed on top of the car in front of him, and then hit 3 or more cars, and turned sideways. He could clearly see the driver and the passenger, as it hit more cars. It was the same driver and passenger he had seen in his dream. All the flying debris somehow missed his car as he sat in the very epicenter of a major accident.

He pulled out of the mess without a scratch. If he had been in the truck that he normally drives, it would have been too high for the truck to fly over it.

He pulled over and called the police, described the accident, and the exact location. They told him they were aware of the accident, but he was the first person who could give them the exact location. Then he drove 15 minutes home, and described to his family the whole scene. They had already heard it the day before, as he had related his dream!

The God who Answers Back can sometimes be ahead of the problem, providing the answer before we even ask.

Emmanuel's full testimony can be seen on YouTube: The God Who Answers Back: The Accident that Never Happened: Emmanuel Cibasu (https://bit.ly/3JgmQ1w).

Clarence Mostert

Healed of Deadly Blood Infection

Clarence Mostert, Blood Infection Healed
thegodwhoanswersback@gmail.com

80 year old Clarence Mostert was stunned with a sudden affliction that had him hovering near death. All of a sudden, he could not get out of bed, in fact, he could barely move. They rushed him to the hospital for tests, but the problem was elusive. The reason for his condition was a mystery to the doctors who examined him.

He was sent home, but that night an urgent phone call

from the hospital came in. Clarence had to come immediately to the hospital to receive antibiotics for a deadly blood infection. They first tried one type of antibiotics, but then switched to another and his body reacted violently, rejecting the antibiotics. The type of infection Clarence had was serious, and patients can die very quickly. The doctors again were puzzled, and thought perhaps it was a gall bladder problem, and it would need to be removed. The experts were flailing for options. That was the situation on Saturday night.

But Sunday morning, the church prayed for Clarence, and from that moment, everything changed. Monday morning Clarence was perfectly fine and went home with no trouble at all! And the gall bladder operation? — it never happened.

Clarence and his wife Audrey tell the whole story on YouTube: The God Who Answers Back: Healed of Blood Infection: Clarence Mostert (https://bit.ly/3vrLpTA).

Abigail Elise Tushner

Infertility Healed

"My wife and I were married in the fall of 2013 and both longed to have a family. After around 5 years with no child, we began to see different specialist to see what we could do and, after many doctors' appointments, weren't given a lot of hope. Several supernatural events took place in the span of 2-3 years where God would give us assurance that the promise was for us, and that barrenness would not last.

"One such event was in the fall of 2019. We were having special meetings and the guest minister, Brother Ron Spencer, was preaching on "Take it Back." During the sermon, he was walking past my aisle and as he passed by, he turned back to tell me "The baby is on the way." A few weeks later as my wife and I were discussing that event, we were talking about how good God was in giving us the promise and we were wondering will we have twins?—will it be one?—and just wondering what was in store for us. During the conversation, the most beautifully bright shooting star shot across the sky in front of us and just seemed to be one more confirmation that God was at work.

"So many in our church were praying for us and encouraging us to stay strong in the faith. Our pastor, during a trip to Israel, had a very special prayer in Shiloh where the Bible tells us the story of Hannah and her desire to have a child. We knew that God had everything in control, and we kept the faith and believed that no matter the report, we would see the promise fulfilled.

"The summer of 2021 we got the news that my wife was pregnant and on Good Friday of 2022, our little Abigail Elise Tushner was born. She was 6 pounds, 13 ounces of joy and happiness. Abigail meaning, "a Fathers Joy." Elise meaning "God's promise." She is healthy, happy, and has brought such joy in our lives. We thank God every day that He never left us alone and He is faithful to His word."

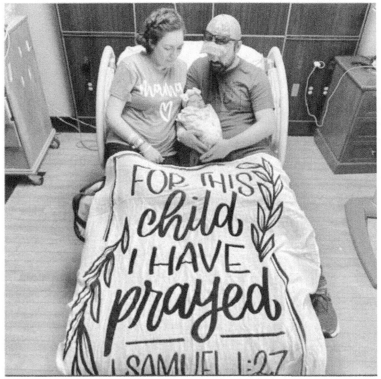

Andrew and Candace Tushner, with baby Abigail

Jason DeMars

Covid at its Worst

We all know that Covid 19 does not hit everyone the same. For some it is mild, for others, deadly. Jason DeMars' episode was the deadly kind.

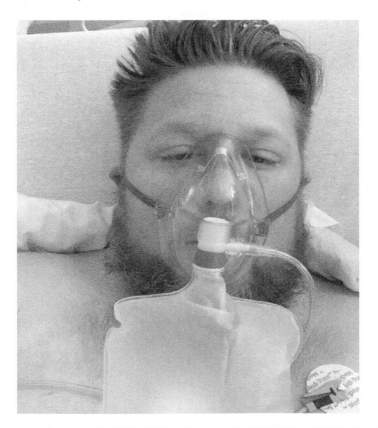

He was in the hospital, unconscious, powerless to help himself, completely unaware of his surroundings or visitors, and his blood oxygen count was dangerously low. This was a classic case where the cemetery is often the next destination. Medical science was doing all it could, but the situation was grim.

Then the God Who Answers Back intervened. Jason DeMars has worked as a missionary, and is known around the world. A prayer chain was started, and requests went out to his friends around the world. The recovery that followed was nothing short of miraculous.

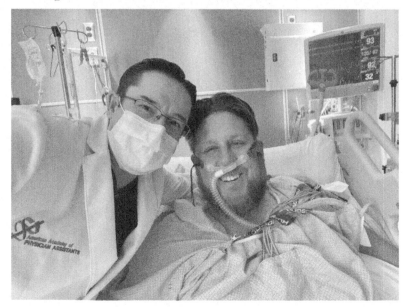

Jason DeMars has his own YouTube channel under his name, and you can hear him tell the whole story there under the title: Testimony of Deliverance (https://bit.ly/3oFEnab).

Real Miracles as Reported by Everyday People

Fanny Crosby

The Miracle of Faithfulness

Real Miracles as Reported by Everyday People

Sometimes the greatest miracle is not a healing, but the testimony of someone who remains faithful to God when they don't receive a miracle. Fanny Crosby composed some of the world's most beloved hymns, such as Great is Thy Faithfulness, Pass me not Oh Gentle Savior, and To God be the Glory. Over her lifetime, she composed over 8000 hymns and gospel songs. Surely, such inspiration is evidence of a deep and enduring faith. However, for her entire life, Fanny Crosby was blind. She went to her savior to receive her sight, where His face would be the first thing she would ever behold.

Growing old unto death is the greatest sickness of all—no one escapes it. But Salvation reverses that, with the gift of Eternal Life paid for by the sacrificial death of Jesus Christ on Calvary. Therefore, physical healing is included in the atonement, whether it happens in this life or the next.

Sometimes, for His own sovereign purposes, God allows an affliction to continue throughout a person's life. In those cases, another miracle takes place: The Miracle of trust, and faithfulness. We salute and honor those like Fanny Crosby, who provide this wonderful testimony of faith.

Todd Reier

A Life of Miracles

Todd and Stephanie Reier

"I was raised in a Lutheran church. My mother took me to a church camp in the mountains by Glacier National Park, where I witnessed a supernatural healing. After going forward for prayer, I witnessed a man who had one leg shorter than the other who also went forward for prayer. His leg grew 2" in front of my eyes.

"I was born with an ear defect, and was in and out of

hospitals. The Lord miraculously healed my ear defect when I was a child, and I went on to become a musician, playing guitar and singing in bars.

"I had a vague faith from my childhood but no personal walk with God. In 2013, God came into my life in a dramatic way, and I discovered there was a whole new level. God has been very close to me ever since.

"Early this year (2022), I sprained my ankle severely. It might even have been broken, but I limped to church, rather than going to the doctor. It swelled to the size of a tennis ball, and could take no weight at all. At that service, I limped up and sang a special song for the congregation. At the end of the service, the ministers prayed for my ankle, and helped me back to my car. By the next morning, all the swelling was completely gone, and I had not one tiny twinge of pain in that ankle.

"This year (2022) I was diagnosed with cancer. The spot was on my nose, and it looked exactly like pictures of cancer as can be seen on the internet. The biopsy confirmed it. That very week, some Believers with faith that God can heal prayed for me, specifically that the cancer would "turn to dust." Within 15 minutes, the spot literally fell off my nose—like dust!

With all of these experiences, I am absolutely certain that God can and does heal."

Anndrea Grant

Spot found in X-ray Disappears

"My name is Anndrea Grant and I live in Lynden, Washington. I want to give this testimony for the glory of God and to testify that He is the same yesterday, today and forever.

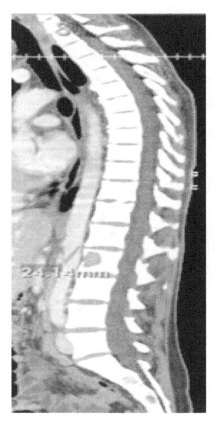

"Around the end of April 2022, I caught a head cold and developed a bad cough. After coughing hard for several days, I started to experience pain on my left side. I had an x-ray which showed a suspicious spot on my left lower rib, so I was immediately sent to my oncologist for further evaluation due to my history of breast cancer. The Lord had miraculously healed me of breast cancer in 2016 and

I have been healthy and normal ever since. Even though I was facing another trial of my faith, I was holding on to all that the Lord had done for me and believing that He is *"the same yesterday, today and forever"* Hebrews 13:8.

"The next day I was in a store and there was a desk calendar on the counter. It was a daily Bible verse desk calendar flipped open to this scripture: *"I am the Lord, who heals you."* Exodus 15:26. I knew this was God speaking directly to me! I was so startled that I physically felt myself jump and I started crying right there in the store. It was so striking and unusual to see a desk calendar with Bible verses on a storekeeper's desk, and for it to be flipped over to a verse about healing when it was so much on my mind.

Later that evening, I went to church for our Wednesday night service. I went up for prayer and at the end of his prayer, my pastor told me to "just go thanking the Lord for it now." I started thanking the Lord out loud right then. Immediately I felt the presence of the Lord almost like He was standing directly in front of me, and I felt that He came in that moment to hear my praise and thanksgiving for my healing.

At the appointment with my oncologist, she told me it was

very probable that the lesion was a recurrence of my previous breast cancer, which would be metastatic breast cancer. She said she would need a biopsy to confirm this diagnosis, but I would have to have a CT scan first to know where to biopsy. Before my CT scan was done, one of my daily devotions used this scripture: *"Wherefore lift up the hands which hang down, and the feeble knees; and make straight paths for your feet, lest that which is lame be turned out of the way; but let it rather be healed."* Hebrews 12:12-13.

"My CT scan test results showed multiple suspicious spots in my ribs and also my spine. The largest of the spots was 2.5cm in my spine and they wanted to schedule a biopsy of this area right away. They also wanted me to get a nuclear medicine bone scan to confirm the CT findings. I had the bone scan on Friday, July 1st. The morning of my bone scan my devotion was about God being victorious in battle and used this scripture: *"Having spoiled principalities and powers, He made a show of them openly, triumphing over them in it."* (Colossians 2:15) The devotion went on to say: *"Our triumph has already been won by our Leader Jesus Christ, but we must identify ourselves with His victory. Stand your ground in the day of battle, and having fought to the end, remain victors on the field!"*

"That evening, after the bone scan was over, our nightly devotion was along the same lines: *"Because the hand of Amalek is against the throne of the LORD."* (Exodus. 17:16) *"In the midst of the throne . . . a Lamb as it had been slain."* Revelations 5:6. *"Arise, O LORD, disappoint him, cast him down."* (Psalms 17:13)

"The next day, we got the test results back from the bone scan: **AND THE 2.5 CM LESION WAS GONE!!!!!!!**

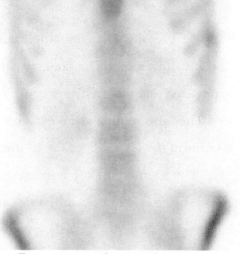

Bone scan—the spot is gone.

"It had completely disappeared! The nuclear medicine bone scan images showed the absence of any lesions in my spine. Because of these test results, my oncologist told me to cancel the bone biopsy because there was nothing to biopsy anymore!

"The Lamb that was slain is now the Mighty Conqueror over death, hell, the grave and cancer!!!! It is a finished work of Calvary and I know I am completely healed from metastatic breast cancer. I pray that all who hear this testimony will know that *"Jesus Christ is the same yesterday, today and forever!"* (Hebrews 13:8)"

Jonas Schumacher

Cancer at 19 years old!

Cancer was the last thing on the mind of young Jonas Schumacher when he went to the doctor for a check up on some bruised ribs he got in a soccer game. The doctor felt around the area and told him his ribs were fine, but casually mentioned that his spleen was elevated, he should get that checked. Jonas thought nothing of it; he had always been healthy, but he still had some routine tests and blood work done.

So when the clinic called and told him he needed to go to the hospital RIGHT NOW, he was puzzled. He felt just fine. But his white blood cell count was at 120,000 units when 5 to 10,000 is normal. These high levels usually meant there was some form of cancer in the blood. All Jonas' plans changed at that moment. He was urged to go directly to the hospital, but he went home until the next day.

He began reading the Bible, and immediately felt at peace. His family and church began praying for him. Jonas spent 10 days in the hospital, and was diagnosed with CML, a type of Leukemia based on a defective chromosome. His condition was chronic, but if not treated soon enough, it would turn from chronic to acute, at which point there would be no medical hope. He was prescribed treatment by chemotherapy, through pills. The bump in the ribs was the first miracle, allowing the cancer to be discovered in time, and it turned out there was nothing wrong with his spleen.

The medication had about a 50 percent chance of working,

but a side-effect of severe itching over his whole body developed, which was intolerable. The cancer was invisible, but the itching was right out in the open. Jonas asked a minister to pray for the itching to stop, and it stopped immediately. That gave Jonas faith to believe that God would heal the cancer also. The treatment began working and eventually, all his levels went back to normal. The whole ordeal took 2 1/2 years.

Jonas testifies that he experienced God's healing in two different ways: instantaneous miraculous healing, which stopped the itching—and medical treatment over time, which cured the cancer.

God heals through medicine as well as through prayers, and prayers can help the medicine to work.

Drew Dexter

"Go get your son! — I just saw a vision of Drew walking."

"Our son, Drew, was born in February 2014, a healthy baby with no complications. But as Drew grew older, he never did crawl. He seemed very weak in his arms and legs. By one year old, he still was not walking or crawling.

"We had to carry Drew everywhere we went. That summer, we had our annual family camp and Brother Ron Spencer was a speaker there. We put Drew in his pajamas that night and put him to bed in our cabin by the church, using a phone as a baby monitor. As the service went on, Brother Ron felt to call a prayer line. When we came forward to be prayed for, Brother Ron asked where Drew was. We told him that he was already sleeping, to which Brother Ron replied, "Run and get him. It will be worth it!" He later told us, "I just saw a vision of Drew walking."

"Drew was prayed for that night and we believed for a complete healing. We saw strength coming to his legs. Several months later, at 18 months old, he was able to hold onto furniture and walk stiff-legged around it. He still couldn't pull up and couldn't take steps on his own but we knew the Lord had started a work.

"That August, Sister Karen Pruitt had a brain bleed and came home from the hospital with very poor vision. We were staying at the Pruitt's home as we worked on building our own house and Sister Karen had to spend most of her time simply lying in her bed. With her vision so poor and battling episodes of severe dizziness, she frequently required help just to get up. One day, we placed Drew on the floor at the end of her bed so he could be in the room with her. It wasn't long before the spirit of the Lord swept over the room and Sister Karen lifted her hands and began praising the Lord. At the same time, Drew pushed himself up from the floor and began to walk all around the house! It was truly miraculous and we knew that our many prayers had been answered.

"Although Drew was still unsteady on his feet, we knew that a vision was seen of him walking and if the Lord started a work, He would finish it. Today, Drew's balance has continued to improve, and he is now a fast runner. In fact, his favorite animal is a Cheetah because of how fast they are and Drew claims he is "Cheetah fast."

"His life has been a testimony to many and we are thankful for the Lord's healing touch in his life."

Michael Dexter and Family

Beth Dingwall

A Leukemia with a 100% Fatality Rate—Until Now

Beth was only 8 years old when she was stricken with the deadly form of leukemia known as "Philadelphia positive." There is no known cure.

Beth went to the hospital for tests after feeling sick and not getting better, and it was discovered that her red blood cell count was at 3.5. A normal count would be 12 to 13, and the doctors told her father that this was the first time they had seen a number of less than 4 on a living person. The tests also revealed that 97% of the cells in her bone marrow were cancerous and that 56% of the cells in her blood stream were cancerous as well. With these staggering numbers, the doctors could not understand why she was still alive. Beth's heart rate was 185 bpm, with accompanying high blood pressure. The doctors thought Beth might have days or weeks to live. In the 419 cases of this disease, studies gave her a 0% chance of survival.

Beth's family and church began to pray for Beth. What followed was 3 years of very extensive chemotherapy. During this time, Beth was undergoing many painful tests and procedures including a lumber puncture test every 2 weeks. Beth would make shrilling screams every time this test was performed because of the pain it caused.

The heavy doses of chemotherapy caused Beth to lose her hair many times. It is not uncommon for the hair to grow back a different color and texture—if it grows back at all. But Beth's prayer was that her hair would remain the same.

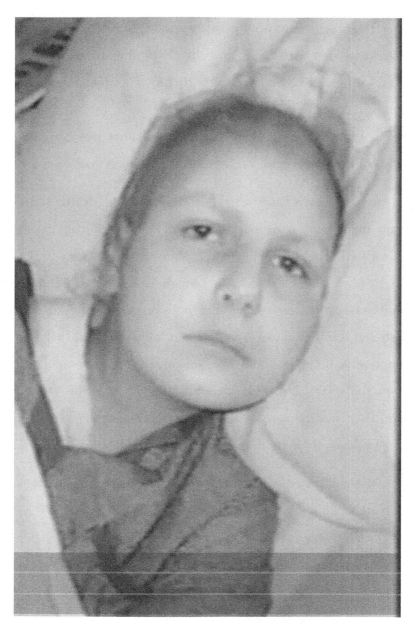

Real Miracles as Reported by Everyday People

After the first 6 months of treatment, Beth's cancer went into remission for 3 years and the chemotherapy treatments were stopped. But 9 months after that, Beth's cancer was back with the same devastating numbers she had at the beginning: 97% of the cells in her bone marrow were cancerous as well as 56% of her blood cells. Zero progress had been made.

Over the next three years, Beth hovered near death. There were many times when Beth's family did not know from day to day if Beth would continue to live. Many times, she was carried to the hospital in the middle of the night by her father, her limp body ravaged by high fever. The only suggestion the doctors had was a bone marrow transplant, a long-shot idea that was impossible on many counts. No one in the family was a match for a transplant. The odds of finding a match was 1 in 100,000 and then that person had to be healthy and willing to be a donor. Even then, the transplant would very likely not take.

Miraculously, a donor was found 5,000 miles away that was a match, who was healthy and willing to be a donor. The transplant procedure was performed, but would it take? They would know in three days, for that is the longest the cells would survive. For 10 straight days, Beth's white blood cell count remained at zero. Nothing was happening, all hope was gone, and death was imminent.

Then, one night, Jesus came into the room. Beth actually saw him, physically. Beth describes it as a hazy white heavy atmosphere that made it difficult to move or talk. This presence was so full of love and peace. She became aware that someone was walking at the end of the bed, and He came around the side of the bed to stand on the opposite side of the bed from where her mother was sitting. Beth knew it was the Lord Jesus. He put his arm around her shoulders, and Beth could feel herself sitting up. The Lord took her hand and was smiling.

The next day, miraculously, Beth's white blood cell count began to rise! The doctors had said it would take 6 months for Beth's numbers to go back to normal. Not this time. After 3 more days, Beth was doing so well, she was released from the hospital, and a swift and full recovery followed.

Normally a person enduring all of this would have ongoing health problems, but Beth has had none of those. Beth is a healthy and thriving young woman today, an assistant elementary school teacher with beautiful brown curly hair!

Today, there are some clinical trial treatments that are showing promise of treating Philadelphia Positive. But when Beth recovered, she was the ONLY KNOWN CASE in the world who had survived it.

Beth's whole story can be viewed on YouTube: The Beth Dingwall Miracle (https://bit.ly/3bv3dXg).

Beth Dingwall Today

Ron Spencer

A Battle with Cancer in Progress

In this book, we tell the happy endings of some marvelous stories, but in this chapter, we share a work in progress. Pastor and evangelist Ron Spencer has experienced a number of dramatic healings in his own life. He is, in fact, a walking miracle. His prayers have also been used by God to heal many. Now Ron has been attacked with cancer, and has been defying all the prognostications for going on two years. Here is one excerpt from a sermon he preached on July 30, 2022 titled, *"In a Mess":*

"We shall fight on the beaches, we shall fight on the landing ground, we shall fight in the fields and in the streets, we shall fight in the hills, we shall NEVER SURRENDER!! We will fight for our families, We will fight for our children, we will fight for our healing, we will fight for our deliverance, we will fight for our joy, we will fight for our peace, we will fight for the Holy Ghost! We will fight until our bodies are changed, we will fight till we are sitting at the Marriage Supper of the Lamb!"

This passage perfectly sums up the tenacious spirit and bulldog faith that God has placed within the heart of Rev. Ron Spencer, who has been defeating stage four metastatic cancer since December of 2020. As he continually states, *"I will NEVER quit or surrender!"* While the avenger is on his path daily, God's servant and pastor of a thriving church in Virginia entered the city of refuge many years ago. As Ron often states, *"While Satan decided that he would bombard my body with cancer, he couldn't do it unless he first got permission from God."*

Prior to his diagnosis of cancer, the Lord spoke these words to his heart, *"If you will trust me, I'll use you like never before."* In December of 2020, **he was given only four months to live.** This was his physician's diagnosis, but God had a different report. Today, going on two years later, Ron Spencer continues to preach with more fire than ever, tearing down Satan's kingdom and astonishing medical science. His message is still the same as it has been for decades, God still saves, and God still heals. Jesus Christ is the SAME, yesterday, TODAY, and forever (Hebrews 13:8).

Currently, Ron has multiple brain tumors, his lungs are full of cancer, and it has metastasized to his lymph nodes. Additionally, it has affected several different organs and destroyed his pancreas and adrenal glands. He takes chemotherapy two times a day and about 20 other supportive drugs. He continues to endure repeated brain surgeries, eight shots a day, numerous invasive tests, seizures, severe nausea and vomiting, and pain, with never a day off. Yet, even his physicians have to give glory to God and say, "he is a walking miracle," as hundreds of their other patients have passed away while Ron has lived on. There is no other explanation but God. Ron Spencer appears perfectly healthy outwardly, and he preaches with the strength and breath of his youth!

"No matter how big your Goliath is, a small rock in the hand of faith will fly with supersonic speed and bring him crashing to his knees in defeat," Ron reminds us.

We all have an appointed time to die, but this soldier of the cross will not go quietly into the night. He is a warrior and a living testimony, a Time-Tested Memorial that we serve a living God who still heals!

The stories of some of Ron's past miraculous recoveries can be viewed on YouTube:

Through the Fire: The Testimony of Ron Spencer (https://bit.ly/3Jr2jYk) **-** The story of how Ron survived the explosion of a propane tank at close range.

Brother Ron Spencer: Forty Foot Fall (https://bit.ly/3Jw63HO) - Ron had an accident in which he fell from a tall ladder and crushed the bones in his back. He was told he would never walk again. He walked out of the hospital shortly after that.

Ron and Connie Spencer

Author Owen Jorgensen

Healed of Bursitis

Owen Jorgensen is well known as the author of the Supernatural Biography Series, which covers the life and ministry of the renowned evangelist, William Branham, whose prayers God used to heal many. But while writing about the miracles in the Branham campaigns, Owen himself became afflicted with a serious case of Bursitis, which made his arm almost useless. For a year he suffered with this, and all the best treatments of his doctor provided no answer. Then God reached through time! As Owen was listening to a recorded William Branham service from the 1950's, his faith was inspired, and God provided Owen a miraculous answer that the doctors could not!

Owen's testimony can be viewed on YouTube: The God Who Answers Back: Author Owen Jorgensen Healed of Bursitis (https://bit.ly/3PNdrkF).

Owen Jorgensen's Biography series can be ordered from www.bcfresourcecenter.com.

Dear friend,

We hope the testimonies in this little book have inspired you to consider that the miracle-working God of the Bible is still performing miracles today. Perhaps you are in a state of desperate need yourself. Perhaps not—but maybe, one day you will be. We are all marching toward the grave, and will face our moment, someday. If everyone were ALWAYS healed, no one would ever die. But sometimes, death comes knocking on the door when it is not necessarily our time to die. For those cases, the God Who Answers Back can change things. And your encounter with Him may result in the greatest miracle of all—the salvation of your soul. This blessed miracle comes with the most sublime benefit of all: Eternal life in the world to come, where death is no longer a possibility. Whether you are healed this life or not, every mortal person needs that miracle—and it is freely available to those who ask.

We firmly believe that the Bible is the source of truth. A balanced and well-developed understanding of the teaching of the Bible on Divine Healing is extremely helpful in receiving your own healing. It also is a safe-guard against fanaticism.

Real Miracles as Reported by Everyday People

Healing is not just a possibility, it is in fact the will of God, in many situations. As F.F. Bosworth pointed out, "Faith begins where the will of God is known." And when faith arises, amazing things happen. The resources below have helped others develop the faith to approach God with their request, and receive an answer.

Recommended Resources

- "Christ the Healer" by F. F. Bosworth. An in-depth discussion of the Biblical case for Divine Healing. Available from many sources.

- For more evidence of a miracle-working God who is active today, we recommend the series "Supernatural: The Life of William Branham" by Owen Jorgensen. Available from www.bcfresourcecenter.com.

- For faith-inspiring quotes, read "Healing Thoughts." Selected excerpts from the sermons of William Branham. Available from www.bcfresourcecenter.com.

- The website: www.alivinggod.com has a good collection of testimonies, including some that are in this book.

- Subscribe to **thegodwhoanswersback** (https://bit.ly/3bfEyWC) channel on YouTube for more testimonies.

You can always contact us at:
thegodwhoanswersback@gmail.com

Do You Need Prayers?

Submit a request at:

www.thegodwhoanswersback.org

Send Email to:

thegodwhoanswersback@gmail.com

If you are not in our area, we have partnering ministries all around the world. Contact us for a referral.

Other Books by Mark Aho

- The Solomon's Bride Series: A Biblical Love Story Dramatized - https://amzn.to/3Q1sM14, and www.bcfresourcecenter.com